Find It in Nature!

Animal Homes

by Jenna Lee Gleisner

Bullfrog Books

Ideas for Parents and Teachers

Bullfrog Books let children practice reading informational text at the earliest reading levels. Repetition, familiar words, and photo labels support early readers.

Before Reading

- Discuss the cover photo. What does it tell them?

- Look at the picture glossary together. Read and discuss the words.

Read the Book

- "Walk" through the book and look at the photos. Let the child ask questions. Point out the photo labels.

- Read the book to the child, or have them read independently.

After Reading

- Prompt the child to think more. Ask: Have you seen an animal home? What did it look like? What animal lived in it?

Bullfrog Books are published by Jump!
5357 Penn Avenue South
Minneapolis, MN 55419
www.jumplibrary.com

Library of Congress Cataloging-in-Publication Data

Names: Gleisner, Jenna Lee, author.
Title: Animal homes / by Jenna Lee Gleisner.
Description: Minneapolis, MN: Jump!, Inc., [2025]
Series: Find it in nature! | Includes index.
Audience: Ages 5–8
Identifiers: LCCN 2024023384 (print)
LCCN 2024023385 (ebook)
ISBN 9798892136693 (hardcover)
ISBN 9798892136709 (paperback)
ISBN 9798892136716 (ebook)
Subjects: LCSH: Animals—Habitations—Juvenile literature.
Classification: LCC QL756 .G563 2024 (print)
LCC QL756 (ebook)
DDC 591.56/4—dc23/eng/20240621
LC record available at https://lccn.loc.gov/2024023384
LC ebook record available at https://lccn.loc.gov/2024023385

Editor: Katie Chanez
Designer: Molly Ballanger

Photo Credits: Roman Pyshchyk/Shutterstock, cover; pathiphan/Shutterstock, 1; DuqueDamian/Shutterstock, 3; Gregory Henry/Dreamstime, 4; wwing/iStock, 5; Malgorzata Surawska/Shutterstock, 6–7; Mircea Costina/Shutterstock, 8–9; Betty4240/iStock, 10–11, 23bl; A_Lesik/Shutterstock, 12, 23tr; Sokolov Alexey/Shutterstock, 13; Oxford Scientific/Getty, 14; Mirebel/Shutterstock, 14–15, 23tl; All-stock-photos/Shutterstock, 16–17; rogelson/Shutterstock, 17; benedek/iStock, 18, 23br; Remi Masson/Nature Picture Library, 19; Nuwat Phansuwan/Shutterstock, 20–21; Shutterstock, 22; Platoo Studio/Shutterstock, 24.

Printed in the United States of America at Corporate Graphics in North Mankato, Minnesota.

Table of Contents

Do not touch!
Never touch an animal home. Keep your distance. This keeps you and animals safe.

Safe Inside

nest

We walk in a forest.
I see a nest in a tree!

A bird lives in the nest.
Her eggs are safe in it.

egg

5

Animal homes are all around.

Let's find more!

This nest hangs in a tree.

It is gray.

It is a wasp's nest!

Wasps fly in and out.

log ····▶

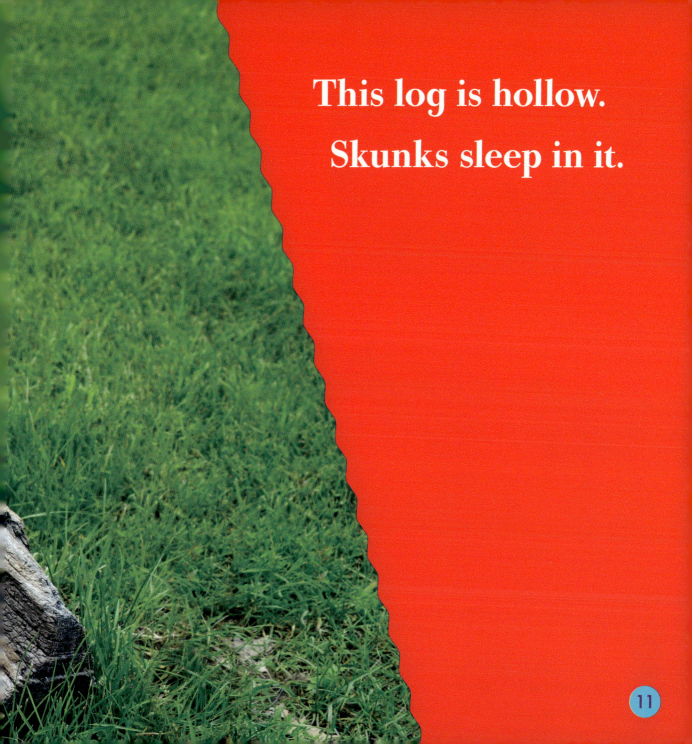

This log is hollow.
Skunks sleep in it.

11

Look at the hill.

See the hole?

It is a den.

den

Foxes live in it!

13

What is in this hole?

A burrow!

Rabbits are safe inside.

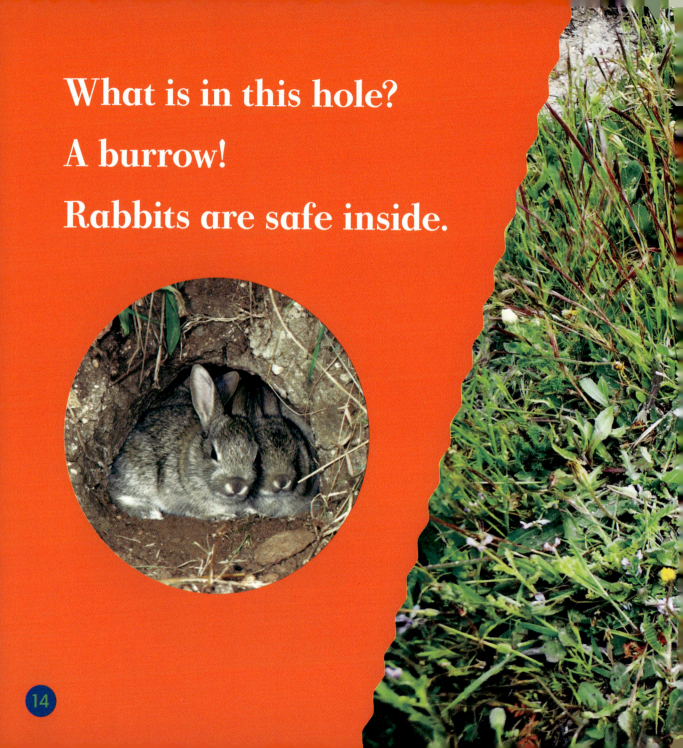

burrow

Bats hang.
They sleep.
Where?
A cave!

cave

17

Look at the water.

The pile of sticks is a home.

It is a beaver lodge!

A beaver swims in.

Homes keep animals safe.

Have you seen one?

Where was it?

Match the Home

Match each animal with its home. Look back at the book if you need help!

Picture Glossary

burrow
A tunnel or hole in the ground made or used as a home by a rabbit or other animal.

den
The home of a wild animal, such as a fox.

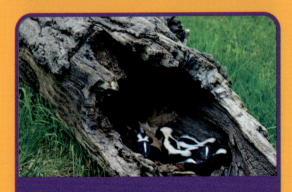

hollow
Empty inside.

lodge
A home in water that beavers build with sticks and mud.

Index

To Learn More

Finding more information is as easy as 1, 2, 3.

❶ Go to www.factsurfer.com

❷ Enter "animalhomes" into the search box.

❸ Choose your book to see a list of websites.